BMX Moves

Edited by Richard Grant and
Nigel Thomas
Editors BMX Action Bike Magazine

Design: Maria Gilbert

Publishing Co-ordinator :
Campbell Goldsmid

Photography: Tim Leighton-Boyce

Printed by Cambus Litho in
Great Britain

Designed and produced by
Autumn Publishing Ltd, 10 Eastgate
Square, Chichester, Sussex and
BMX Action Bike Magazine, 139
Tooley Street, London SE1 2HZ.

Specially produced for
Scholastic Publications Ltd

This book is sold subject to the condition that it shall not, by way of
trade or otherwise, be lent, re-sold,
hired out or otherwise circulated
without the publisher's prior con-
sent in any form of binding or cover
other than that in which it is pub-
lished and without a similar condition, including this condition,
being imposed upon the subse-
quent purchaser.

Scholastic

© UKBMX Publications, 1985
All rights reserved
ISBN 0 590 70551 2

Contents

KT-197-877

BMX moves

This book takes you one stage closer to the raddest sport in the world. BMX. Those three letters stand for bicycle moto-cross. But they also mean the most fun it is possible to have on a bike.

The thrills and excitement of BMX have made it the world's fastest growing cycle-sport. In the 15 short years since the first ramshackle BMX bikes were invented, nearly 20 million have been sold. Wherever you go in the world you'll find boys and girls riding BMX. Some will be at the top of the sport. These are the professionals who ride, race and stunt BMX full-time. They started by being among the thousands of weekend racers.

And then there are the millions who just mess about on their bikes, sprinting and stunting. But they all have one thing in common. They are all having fun.
And that's what BMX Moves is about. Getting more fun from your bike.

Getting air is part of BMX. Most riders fly over jumps. But floating over flat ground is more difficult. This rider only managed it once.

You wouldn't be a normal BMX owner if at some time you didn't want to work on your bike. Part of the fun of owning a BMX is the things you can do to it. The one pictured here is a standard BMX machine. You can ride it, race it and trick it. With a few extra parts it can become a trick freestyle machine. Or stripped down to a lightweight racer. Or you can leave it as it is. It will fit you whether you're seven or 17. All it requires are some simple adjustments. It helps , of course, to know what the various parts do. And what they're called. Otherwise you'll end up walking into a bike shop asking for 'wotsits that do wotsitname...'

Seat: *Made from hard plastic so you can stand as well as sit on it.*

Seatclamp: *Makes a tight connection between the seatpost and frame.*

Wheels: *Racers use alloys like these. Freestylers prefer plastic mags*

Tyres: *Smooth tyre treads work best on the road, large knobblies on mud and small pattern treads in sand.*

Pedals: *Freestylers use wide platforms with small studs, racers prefer cages with sharp teeth.*

Brake lever: *Shaped for one finger operation. It pulls the cable that works the brake.*

Handlebars: *Reinforced with an H-shape and available in heights from six to 10 inches.*

Gooseneck and stemclamp: *The heart of the steering. The four-bolt clamp secures the bars to the forks.*

Radpads: *Protect you from the bike. You must have them on the top-tube and the stemclamp if you want to race.*

Hubs: *The smoothest wheels roll on sealed bearing hubs that keep water and mud out.*

Cranks and chain-wheel: *Transmits your pedal power to the wheels. One piece chrome-moly ones withstand most thrashing. The bigger you are, the longer crank you need.*

5

The best BMX bike is a new one. And the best way to keep your BMX bike like new is to look after it. Maintaining a bike in mint condition is easy. All you have to do to keep it shiny new is clean it regularly and once a week--or after every thrash session-- go round tightening up all the nuts and bolts. Those few minutes work will give you a bike that will last for years.

Check

- Cranks
- Pedal spindles
- Bottom bracket
- Brake shoes
- Lubricate moving parts

Weekly maintenance checklist

Tighten

- Wheel nuts
- Brake lever screws
- Seat clamp
- Seatpost clamp
- Stem bolts
- Steering headset

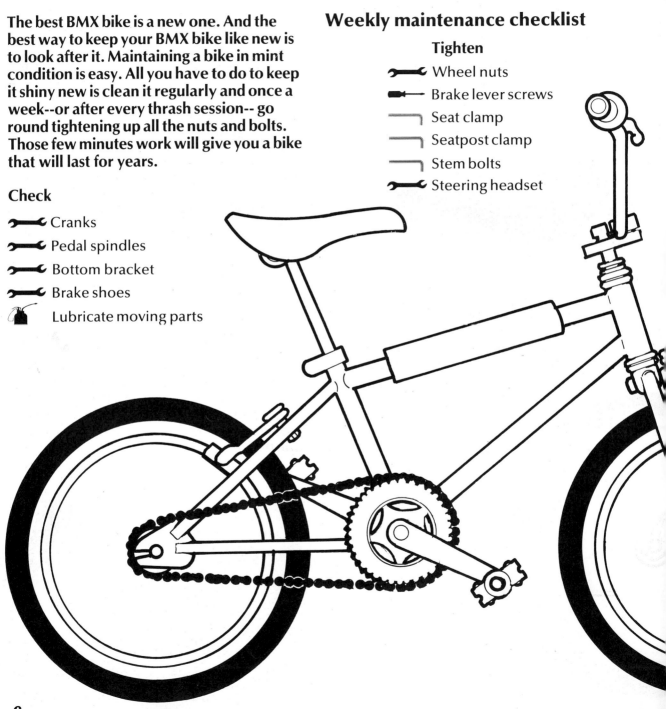

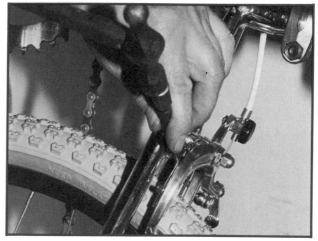

The headset makes sure the bike steers precisely. To check it is not loose put the front brake on and rock the bike back and forward. If you can feel movement, the headset bearings are loose. Use an adjustable spanner to loosen off the locknut, then turn the threaded bearing race beneath until it is handtight. Then loosen it off a quarter turn. Now re-tighten the locknut making sure the threaded bearing race has not tightened further.

Sometimes brake shoes do not close evenly. One brake touches the rim before the other. You can adjust it by lightly tapping the spring on the opposite side with a screwdriver and hammer. This will centre the brakes.

To maximise stopping power and get rid of nasty squeaks 'toe-in' the brake shoes. Use an adjustable spanner to grip the brake caliper and gently bend it. The brake shoe should now be angled so that its leading edge (the one near the front of the bike) is closer to the rim than the back.

BMX is a contact sport. Whether you are a top race pro, a hot freestyler or a raw beginner you will sometimes fall off your bike. But you can avoid being hurt if you wear the correct gear. Essential are a crash helmet, a long sleeve jersey or arm protectors, jeans and trainers. Better still is real BMX protective gear like this. It is designed to be light, hardwearing and cushion and protect you when you hit an obstacle or another rider. Plus it makes you look good and that makes you feel more confident.

Helmet
A full-face skidlid like this protects your whole face including your mouth and chin. Otherwise wear a chinguard.

Racepants
Padded at the hips, knee and shin and made from tough light nylon they do not rip as easily as jeans.

8

Gloves

Get a pair with re-inforced protection on the palms. You'll be glad you did.

Raceshirt

The sleeves are specially padded at the elbow.

Shoes

Make sure the soles have a good pattern to grip the pedals.

Training moves

There's nothing to stop you riding as soon as you have hopped out of bed in the morning. But there would not be much point. You would be stepping on a tuned up bike with an out of tune body. The answer is to get your limbs and joints warmed up and the blood flowing. That doesn't mean you have to do any strenuous exercises or start lifting weights.

One of the best methods of getting your circulation going and tuning up your body is stretching.

It helps your circulation, warms you up, makes you more agile and reduces the risk of muscle strain. And you can do it anywhere.

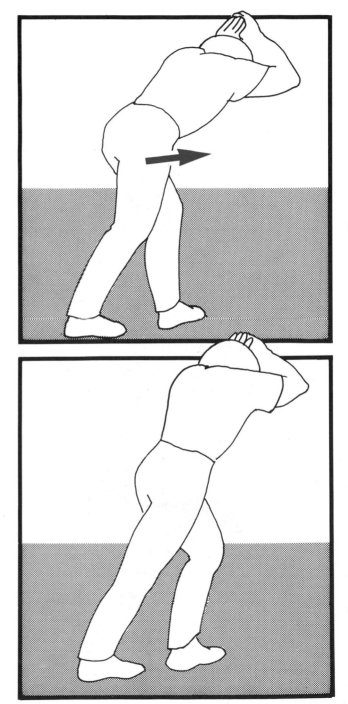

This is an easy exercise to get the calf muscles at the back of your leg in shape.

Find a wall, bend your arms in a V-shape and rest them on the wall. Now lay your head against them. Bend one leg forward beneath you. Leave the other leg straight behind you. Roll your hips forward. Hold it for a few seconds, then relax. Try it with the other leg. Don't overstretch. If it feels painful, you are stretching too far. And breathe normally all the time.

This stretch warms up your upper body, your thigh and calf muscles. They are all key muscles that you use when riding. Plus it helps strengthen the stomach muscles that you use in race starts.

Stand about a foot from a wall with your feet about 10 to 12 inches apart. Stretch your arms back to touch the wall. Now slowly and gently bend forward keeping your legs straight all the time until your fingertips are pointing at the ground. First time out don't expect to touch the ground. The more you stretch, the easier it will become.

You don't always need to go to the gym to lift weights. Pro star Trev Robinson just grabs his team mate Dean Bateson anytime he wants to build up his biceps.

11

Freestyle moves

Freestyle is the BMX sport that you can do anywhere and anytime. All it needs is your bike and you. You don't need a track or people to compete against. Freestyle is about doing what you want to do.

Become hot at freestyle and you become like an acrobat on a bike. You can hop it, flip it, balance it and get air on it. The range of tricks goes on for ever. Freestylers invent new ones each day. Or you can learn tricks like this ramp endo. Do it in easy stages. The first few times work out at ground level. You do not need a ramp or to take your feet off the pedals. As you get more confident , you can add these extra touches that make you more stylish.

NB: When doing freestyle tricks always wear full safety gear and never ride near traffic.

Next to a wheelie there's no more basic freestyle trick than an endo. Master this and it will help when you learn stiffer tricks. All you need is your bike and your safety gear and a place to work out. It helps if you have a kerb to go against, but make sure you work out away from traffic.

1. Pick the spot you plan to endo on. Approach it slowly, head-on, pedals level.

2. As you reach the spot, spring forward so that you shift your weight off the back of the bike.

3. As the back wheel comes off the ground, stretch your arms out to push the bars forward.

4. Still keeping your arms straight, bend your knees and extend your butt back over the bike.

5. The more you push back, the higher the bike will go. Try and let the bike hang up there as long as possible. When you've had enough ease the bike down, backwheel first. Then shift your weight forward and ride away.

5

The Gumbi

They weren't sure what to call this trick, so the freestylers called it a gumbi. But don't bother to look 'gumbi' up in a dictionary. You won't find it. They invented that as well because they could not find any other word to describe it!

17

Fronthops are the next stage on from learning to endo. And fronthops are great to do if you have not got much space to freestyle in. They help you develop balance and once perfected you can invent your own variations like hopping one-handed, one-footed or compete against friends to see who can do the most.

1 Ride forward pedals level, at medium speed.

2 Go into an endo until you reach your balance point.

3 As the bike starts to tip forwards hop the bike up and try to land it on the balance point.

4 Let the bike tip forward again, hop it up then drop the back down. Repeat to keep on hopping.

When you get hot at freestyle, you're rated as rad. Instead of just doing tricks by yourself, you can enter contests and perform before crowds. Start winning and people pay to see you ride. Then you get sponsored by a bicycle company and soon you're touring the world as a freestyle rider. That's the level the riders on these pages have reached. And they have all got there the same way. By non-stop practice.

Eddie Fiola

Since his round-the-world tour Eddie Fiola is now the most famous freestyle entertainer there is. Millions have seen his non-stop acrobatic freestyle routines. These always include Eddie's favourite groundtricks like the pedalscraper, barpress and handstand. And a Fiola act is never complete without Eddie getting rad on a quarterpipe with aerials that clear 10 feet of air

20

Ron Wilkerson

Ron Wilkerson is the king of quickfire freestyle. Everything about him is doublefast. The way he talks, the way he performs. His trick range is as wide as any other freestyler. But his trick rate is twice as fast. And when it includes one-footed one-handed ultra high aerials, 360 frontwheel spins and dropping in *backwards* from the top of a quarterpipe, you can understand how he won the Kellogg's TV freestyle contest.

Neil Ruffell

Neil Ruffell is the newest star in freestyle. Yet until quite recently he was just the unknown younger brother of race star Andy Ruffell. Then Neil shot to stardom by coming from nowhere to second place on TV's Kelloggs' BMX Championship. And since then Neil has become King of the Skateparks. Neil's current best-known trick is the no-handed cherry-picker. But it won't be for long. Neil learns new tricks superfast and he's always inventing new ones.

Craig Campbell

Craig Campbell has scored lots of firsts. He's the first rider ever to double as British Freestyle champion and King of the Skateparks. And the first freestyle rider to have a bike named after him. A supersmooth rider, Craig is famous for his footplants-- split-second foot-on foot-off dabs at the top of the quarterpipe . Footplants require timing and nerves of chrome-moly. And Craig has got them both.

Race moves

If you like excitement, thrills, action and riding fast in a bunch you will love BMX racing.

Local clubs stage novice races for beginners. But if you want to watch the stars in action go to a big national meeting with hundreds of racers.

Big or small , BMX meetings are always run the same way. Riders race in motos of eight according to their age group. In the qualifying motos the same eight race each other three times. The first four overall go through to the next round. Eventually there are just eight riders left for the main event. The winner of this gets a trophy and points towards a No 1 plate.

How BMX races start all over the world: 'Riders Ready, Pedals Ready, Go...!' In BMX racing how you get away often decides how you finish.

Starts are critical in BMX. Snap out the gate one-tenth of a second too late or too early and you blow your chance of winning. That's why top BMX racers practice hundreds of starts each day.

If you haven't got a startgate the best way to practice is to balance against a wall or a lampost. Then imagine the starter is shouting 'Riders Ready, Pedals Ready, Go..!' Better still, get a friend to call the start for you.

1 Nine out of ten riders use the two pedal balance start.
Position your pedals almost flat with the front pedal slightly higher than the back. Breath deep and slow to stay relaxed.

2 Go!!!! The moment the gate starts to drop, snap your weight hard forward so your belt almost hits your bars. Keep your back straight and shoulders back. And crank like crazy.

3 The power of that first pedal should let the bike clear the gate completely. As you come round for the second turn of the pedals shift back into your normal pedalling position.
Demo by: Sid Salisbury. Track: Hounslow.

If you are fast at BMX and win more races than anyone in your age group you get a No 1 plate. Then you might get sponsored like these three famous riders. BMX companies give them bikes, race gear and send them to BMX races all over the world.

Andy Ruffell

Andy Ruffell is the most famous BMX rider in Britain. He's on television and radio, always in magazines and has had a book written all about him. Giant photos of Andy doing BMX tricks are plastered on billboards. Since leav-ing school BMX has been Andy's full-time job.

Most days Andy spends doing freestyle shows before large crowds or training on his racebike. And most weekends he races for money. It's worth it. From BMX Andy has earnt enough to buy his own house and car.

Geth Shooter

You don't have to be into BMX for long before you become a star. Geth Shooter had only been racing a year when he became a hero overnight . It happened when Geth raced on TV against the best riders in the world, the American professionals and beat them all.

David Maw

David Maw is the most successful seven year old BMX racer in the world. Twice a World Champion he's won every No 1 raceplate available in his age group. These include the World Championship he also won when he was six, the European Championship and the British Championship. And his Mum still calls him Soap Dodger.

Speedjumping is the BMX way of riding fast over a steep bump without losing speed or control. It's easy to learn and essential for BMX racing. The trick is to keep your back tyre on the ground all the time. Flying through the air may look rad, but in a race it reduces your speed. And your chances of winning.

Demo rider: Jamie Vince Location: First speed-jump at Hounslow race track

1. As you approach the jump, pull the front wheel up into a power wheelie. Keep pedalling.

3. Once on the lip of the jump, start pushing the front end down. Your bodyweight should be over the back of the bike with your arms fully-stretched.

2. As you reach the jump keep the front wheel as close to the lip as possible without touching it. Start to bend your legs so your whole body is compressed low over the back of the bike.

4. Pull your body back into the power position and crank away.

Winners

BMX race meetings are like one large party that lasts all day. The best moment is often the last moment. After all the excitement comes the celebrations. Time to collect your trophy, grin, laugh and wave at your friends. And find out what they put inside the trophies.